Body Language and Non-verbal Communication

The Ultimate Guide for Reading People. Body Language and Non-verbal Communication Will Have No More Secrets for You.

© Copyright 2021 - All rights reserved.

The content contained within this book may not be reproduced, duplicated or transmitted without direct written permission from the author or the publisher.

Under no circumstances will any blame or legal responsibility be held against the publisher, or author, for any damages, reparation, or monetary loss due to the information contained within this book. Either directly or indirectly.

Legal Notice:

This book is copyright protected. This book is only for personal use. You cannot amend, distribute, sell, use, quote or paraphrase any part, or the content within this book, without the consent of the author or publisher.

Disclaimer Notice:

Please note the information contained within this document is for educational and entertainment purposes only. All effort has been executed to present accurate, up to date, and reliable, complete information. No warranties of any kind are declared or implied.

Readers acknowledge that the author is not engaging in the rendering of legal, financial, medical or professional advice. The content within this book has been derived from various sources. Please consult a licensed professional before attempting any techniques outlined in this book.

By reading this document, the reader agrees that under no circumstances is the author responsible for any losses, direct or indirect, which are incurred as a result of the use of information contained within this document, including, but not limited to, — errors, omissions, or inaccuracies.

Table of Contents

Introduction

The following chapters will discuss the numerous ways to acquire what you want from other people. This book will specifically focus on dark psychology tactics. Here, one is expected to garner enough data on ways you can work with people and use them to your advantage, their innermost desires and emotions being one of the many elements to utilize. Through the mentioned techniques in this book, one is better able to take control and improve the quality of life. Moreover, this book also comprises of several actionable tips that will help you break apart the people in your life and allow you to get ahead of them. Whether you want to use this book for yourself or someone dear to you, it is entirely your choice. Anyone who desires to build and exert their influence over others will find this book to be very helpful.

In addition, this is one of a series of books discussing some of the main points in dark psychology and manipulation. With this at the palm of your hands, you are better able to perform manipulation on either yourself, someone you love, or someone you hate. Whoever it may be, we talked about how to distinguish manipulative tactics from mere deception or coercion properly. You'll learn about the top personalities who devoted their entire life into researching the basic components of the human mind and psychological effects that certain actions may have on an individual.

Today, many books with this subject matter flock the market. That said, it is a pleasure that you have chosen this one. Each effort created guarantees to make sure this book is filled with useful information. Please enjoy!

Chapter 1: Body Language and Non-verbal Communication

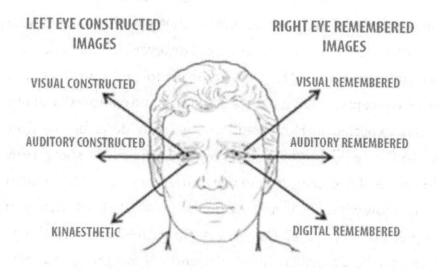

LEFT EYE CONSTRUCTED IMAGES

RIGHT EYE REMEMBERED IMAGES

VISUAL CONSTRUCTED

VISUAL REMEMBERED

AUDITORY CONSTRUCTED

AUDITORY REMEMBERED

KINAESTHETIC

DIGITAL REMEMBERED

Non-verbal communication is a huge part of your life, whether you realize it or not. Each time that you talk to a person, there are tons of messages that are being conveyed through the slightest body movements. When you experience this, you are just talking to the person, and you are listening to what the person is saying, and you are using your mind to connect with them. However, your visual, smell, hearing, and other senses perceive tons of information that is being processed automatically.

Language is a blunt force tool. What is language supposed to do? It is supposed to convey thoughts, ideas, concepts, and stories to other people accurately. It gives us a way to interact and puts us all on one level of communication so that we can make simple messages to each other and get by. However, language is also responsible for transmitting the most important and deep and abstract concepts. What it comes down to is the complexity of our everyday experience. How could you actually describe the flow when you're replaying basketball and making every shot? How could you really describe that in words to someone and have them actually know what you were experiencing? What about when you eat a piece of chocolate? Get broken up with? These are things that cannot be described in words, and yet we try to describe them. Sometimes it is done in ordinary conversation; sometimes, it is done in art or literature.

Language is what mutes and bottlenecks our experience into what we are able to convey to other people. Language is so limited in its ability to truly share our experience with others, and it is that limitedness that makes it, so that body language is so important. You are often experiencing both at them at the same time; you are experiencing someone's language simultaneously with their body language. Non-verbal communication is not all just body language, but a huge part of it is body language.

Think about one interaction that you have had in the last few days. It could be anything from buying something at the store or to a wedding—any tiny little interaction that you had. Try to imagine the interaction from the very beginning.

Body language is comprised mostly of a few factors: affect, posture, and motion. Effect refers to a person's facial expression. If a person is smiling, you could say that they have a bright effect. A person's effect is not always congruent with what they're saying and experiencing. You might see this in someone who is talking nervously about something, and they begin to smile. This means that their expression does not fit whatever they are talking about and that there is incongruence in their effect. When a person has a congruent affect, their facial expressions will change and be malleable. A person who has a congruent and secure affect will be expressing whatever they're thinking about or talking about on their face.

Posture is the way that a person holds himself or herself. This comes from their orientation to the world this can be found in the Enneagram of personality that we talked about earlier. These personality types describe basically an orientation to the world. Some people rear oriented as warriors, others are oriented as perfectionists. The way that a person's personality is will dictate the way they hold themselves physically. A person who is up in their mind will have the posture of a distracted person. A proud person will lead with their chest. What the chest symbolizes is a place of pride. It is where the heart and lungs are, and ties are protected by a cage of bones it is obviously a very important part of our bodies, and when we lead with that, we are showing that we are confident.

What would the chest be doing on a person who did not feel confident? If a person is not confident, they will be not is leading with the chest, rather it will be collapsing. Think about a person who is not confident, and how their shoulders move forward, and their posture seems tired or broken. They are the ones without confined because they are trying to protect their heart.

Another aspect of nonverbal communication is art. When we talk about art in this sense, we are talking about the capital "A" Art that includes sculpture, writing, acting, and all the creative arts. Even when language is involved, it is not verbal communication, it is writing. All of these fall under nonverbal communication. Learning to participate in artistic creation can help you to be a person who is more in touch with this part of communication.

Art can have all kinds of functions. Sometimes its function is to help sell things. This is a form of communication. When you hear something on the radio that is a catchy jingle that makes you feel a certain way about a product that is a deep form of communication. Art can help us to dance, to think, to feel joy or sadness, to help make things clearer, to make political action, to call to war, to call for peace. Music has a variety of functions. It can be used to help us energize or relax. Art is the same way.

Non-verbal communication is happening all the time; you are just not noticing it. Your gaze has a deep implication on how people perceive you the way you walk can tell people a whole lot. A person is a private person when they do not show you much with these.

Some people do not have the power of verbal communication. Some people are people who have very advanced dementia or other mental disorders such as advanced schizophrenia. Others could be people with learning or developmental disabilities like autism or Down syndrome. Can these people still communicate? Absolutely! They can communicate because their lives have revolved around learning ways for them to communicate.

Some ways that it might be easier to communicate with people who are non-verbal are touch, music, art, or hand symbols. People who are non-verbal tend to experience are in a deep way.

Some people have learning or developmental disabilities that prevent them from reading non-verbal cues. People with Autism Spectrum Disorder have a hard time deciphering the cues of behavior and non-verbal communication. ASD is a somewhat mysterious condition, and it is only diagnosed and marked by certain behavioral patterns and lack of social ability. This makes it a fascinating condition to learn how to help people with ASD to function better. In order for kids with ASD to be able to function better, they have to be helped to have integration. This means that they must learn to use their sensory inputs in concordance with their cognitive abilities to learn what a person is expressing. They will have to learn that when a person has their face all scrunched up, and they are yelping, that a person is angry. They have to learn about the body language of a sad person and how to act around that person.

This is pretty much what we are doing in this book, except we are talking about it on higher-level order. Rather than teaching kids how to learn the basic cues of non-verbal communication, we are trying to encourage you to learn to trust your intuition and be able to analyze behavior patterns on a deeper level.

This means that when you experience a behavior pattern, you are able to surmise what this means for you and what it means for other people around you. Instead of thinking about your feeling and worrying about it, you are able to either express it or act on it or do whatever wiles they need to do.

This is where the intuition comes in. you've got to trust what you are feeling about a person. If you see that a person walks into the room with a smile you've known before, and they act a certain way that you saw a person act, and you can know that they are trying to deceive you, this will make your life a little bit easier, as you can have that knowledge going in.

If you start to go to a new church, and at first you like it because of the community, but then you start to feel that it is just not the right place for you, this is intuition. We can use intuition to the behavior patterns of other can know if they will be good partners, good friends, etc.

Let's use the example of dating to try and illustrate what we are talking about when we talk about intuition. A new partner will be a new experience. It will be something that comes to you when you need it. People that we get involved with are generally on the same level of personal development as we are. If they aren't, these will inevitably lead to tension in the relationship. When we get into a romantic relationship with a person, we start to blend together our patterns of behavior. This means that you will seek out a person that will tend to increase the behaviors that you want to increase within yourself.

This is a good and bad thing. It is a natural process that lets us select people to get into relationships with so that we function better in our lives. However, if we are not able to see how we are not functioning well in our lives, then we will just be looking for someone to help us continue the patterns that we already find so easy to do. This is how patterns in relationships are perpetuated.

Chapter 2: The Importance of Reading People

A recap of the previous chapter, we learned how non-verbal communication is sometimes more influential as compared to verbal communication. Moreover, we have also learned some of the basic assumptions of neuro-linguistic programming, most of which talk about the internal and external resources made available to an individual, and how that individual utilizes these resources to achieve their desired outcomes.

Communication has always played a critical role in human interaction. Furthermore, experts have also claimed that communication is mainly non-verbal. Without the necessary internal and external resources used for interpreting body language, the individual will most likely miss the message. Thus, reading people, which takes a massive part in the communication process, should be given utmost importance.

In the previous chapter, it was discussed that one of the presuppositions of NLP was that both good and bad behaviors have a positive intent. Furthermore, the concealed positive plan from bad behavior is known, as one is Secondary Gain. If you genuinely want to understand this book and fully utilize your ability to manipulate people, you must learn how to read people through verbal and non-verbal ways and identify their Secondary

Gain. Once you have identified this as an external resource utilizing your internal resources, you are better able to achieve your desired outcomes. Keep in mind that comprehending the patterns of human behavior and learning body language allows you to view past the façade most people put on. Behind an individual's perfect smile, there ought to be some form of sadness, and reading people using the concepts discussed in this book will allow you to see past through individuals' projection of themselves. Furthermore, by using the underlying concepts of neuro-linguistic programming, you can better gauge the entire process of communication between individuals without being misled by what society deems as merely polite gestures.

In reading people, you must know what they truly feel without relying much on what they actually because, in reality, each one of us lies. Thus, verbal communication cannot guarantee the truth. Without the truth, reading people is a waste of time. You read people so that you can learn about the truth. It is essential that you find out what they are really thinking, what their true thoughts are, and how they feel about a particular situation. If you know the truth, it would be easy for you to understand that person; thus, it would also be easy for you to handle them accordingly and manipulate them.

On another note, it is important to remember that reading people is not possible if you are clinging on to past grudges or biased judgment. You have to let go of all of these misconceptions and prejudices about people before you can genuinely interpret body language as these biases only distort the truth. As a result, you may acquire false assumptions about someone, which will jeopardize your entire process of manipulation. If you want to influence other people's actions, you need to know their true desires. To do this, you need to learn the patterns of human behavior and the secrets of body language.

With that being said, this book aims to guide you through the process of influencing people through verbal and non-verbal cues. It is never easy to read people. More so, it is challenging to analyze people and influence them to perform a certain action that you desire. One must be keen and, as explained earlier, must let go of all of the biases and misconceptions about people.

Chapter 3: Understanding All About Body Language Cues

In this chapter, we will talk about understanding everything there is to learn about body language cues. This is crucial as manipulation heavily relies upon these non-verbal cues. Manipulation is defined as an act of altering the environments to adhere to the characteristics that you want. Thus, to change these environments, you must be able to know the truth first. From here, you employ questionable tricks, such as misdirection, temptation, and distraction, to get what you want. You will learn more about the basics of manipulation in the succeeding chapters. First, look at the chart below to get an idea as to the impact of your communication.

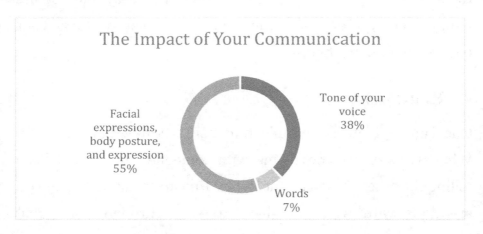

The Impact of Your Communication

Facial expressions, body posture, and expression 55%

Tone of your voice 38%

Words 7%

Functions of non-verbal communication

To read people, you have to rely on both verbal and non-verbal communication. Verbal communication is as direct as it is. However, no one can guarantee that people are always saying the truth every time. With that in mind, those who wish to manipulate and influence people to do specific actions must rely on non-verbal cues to learn more about the other person.

• Complementing

Complementing is done to add credibility, as well as support what has been said. If you are to look at non-verbal communication as something genuine, then the message is strengthened. However, if it were fake, you would doubt the authenticity of the word. When you are happy, a real and genuine smile will complement the actual message that you are satisfied. If you say that you are happy, yet you are not, there is doubt placed upon your confession of being happy.

• Regulating

One can regulate communication using non-verbal language. Whenever you are conversing with someone, you cannot keep telling the other person that it is their time to speak whenever you are done with what you have to say. Through non-verbal language, a person is already able to tell when it is their time to speak.

• Substituting

As the name suggests, substituting allows non-verbal language to take over verbal communication. There is a variety of non-verbal language that is obvious. Whenever someone you do not like is invading your space, you take a step back to say in a non-verbal way that you do not like the fact that they are too close, no words necessary. Even one's facial expressions are clearly non-verbal language that is easily picked up by another person.

• Accenting

Another function of non-verbal language includes accenting. This is used to emphasize your verbal message. A great example would be to hold someone's hands when delivering bad news. When you are disciplining a child, you touch their shoulder as a means to reassure them that you still care for them in spite of the anger you feel at that moment.

Basic body language cues

Most of the time, people would interpret non-verbal cues without ever knowing they are doing it. For example: if you are talking to someone and they suddenly changed their facial expressions, you will be able to pick up on that using your senses. As a result, you will be more careful with what you say next. Depending on what you want to attain, you can read the other person's body language to confirm their true emotions.

Now, in mastering neuro-linguistic programming as a means to manipulate people, you need to start with the basics, and that is reading some of the most common body language cues.

- **Eyes**

Those who have studied NLP would agree to the adage that the eyes are the windows to the soul. You can read another person's true emotions by observing how their eyes move or how fast they blink. Even though the eyes are relatively small as compared to the other body parts, the eyes can create numerous expressions that can reveal the entire truth.

Let us start with telling whether or not a person's way of blinking is normal. You have to assess whether they are blinking too fast or too slow. If someone is anxious about something, they tend to blink fast. Moreover, rapid blinking also indicates that they are telling a lie. On another note, if the person is blinking slowly, it shows that they are trying to control their eye movement. You can assume that they are hiding something or trying to suppress an emotion.

How the eyes move also shows how engaged the other person is in the conversation. Those who show interest in the conversation would rarely break eye contact. If an individual frequently breaks eye contact, they may be distracted or bored. Moreover, it can also mean that they are naturally submissive or may be nervous about conversing with other people. Whenever you are talking to someone whom you are trying to decipher, pay attention to how they glance at certain objects in the room. Anyone who barely maintains eye contact and always glances at their watch or at the door is secretly saying that they wish to end the conversation and leave.

The size of the pupils can also reveal how much a person is interested in the conversation. Now, determining whether or not the other person has dilated pupil can be a bit of a challenge even under the right conditions. Moreover, you have to consider that a dilated pupil may have been affected by light. These are the things you have to consider when trying to decide if a person is genuinely interested. The good news is that you are always allowed to test this out. Remember, the dilation or contraction of one's pupil is automatic, so you have to have a keen eye. Next time you are conversing with someone who appears to be bored, immediately switch the topic into something you know elicits interest from the other person and observe the change in their pupils.

• **Voice**

If we are talking about body language, then it is crucial that we discuss the use of vocalic. It is important to note that vocalic is different from the words that pass a message. Vocalic is all about how people communicate with their voice; this includes the way you open your mouth, the tone of your voice, how loud or soft you are when you are talking, and more. If you pay close attention to another person's vocalic, you will notice certain differences in what they are saying and what their voice is revealing. It is important to note that an individual's voice can change depending on the person they are speaking to, the gender of that person, their level of attractiveness, their social ranking, or even their age. Notice how the voice you use when you speak to your friends is quite different from the voice you use when you speak to your supervisor from work. Moreover, notice how your tone changes when you are talking with someone you like or someone you find attractive.

Even those who are not experts in voices can easily distinguish the vocalic of an individual. Human beings are made to understand paralanguage long before they could also formulate the needed words to communicate. Animals, such as dogs, use paralanguage to respond to their masters' commands. They may not necessarily understand the words, but they are able to understand what the message is through the vocalic of their masters. If you can understand the paralinguistic elements of verbal communication, then you can pretty much manipulate the conversation, and thus, shape the other person. Of course, you also need to master how you would react when conversing with someone. You need to know your strengths and weaknesses and be aware of your vocal strengths. This level of awareness will let you influence others because reading their vocalic gives you the ability to analyze them and their true intentions. Thus, you would like to know how to handle them regardless of what the situation is.

There are six types of vocalic that you should be familiar with — rate, volume, tone, pitch, vocal signature, and rhythm. The rate of speech pertains to how slow or fast the person speaks. With this, you will be able to tell people's emotional state, credibility, and even their intelligence. If you are talking with someone and they answer almost immediately, it goes to show that they are very much assured in what they have to say. On another note, hesitation is a sign that the person is hiding something or is lying about something. They needed the time to form the lies in their head. It is important to note that these rules do not apply in public speaking because the speaker would want to be slow as it means they want to emphasize certain things. If a public speaker talks fast, it may indicate nervousness.

Volume pertains to the audibility of the person's voice. By carefully listening to the vocality of the speaker, you will be able to tell their speech's level of intensity through the volume of their voice. One of the most common myths when it comes to the volume of the voice is that a soft voice always represents humility; this is not always the case. A soft voice can very much radiate intensity, especially when combined with the right tone and facial expression. In fact, a soft voice that has a compelling intensity can be very daunting and may sound threatening. Thus, when considering the volume of the voice, you also need to take into account their tone. The tone helps you assess the emotions behind the speaker's words.

Furthermore, the pitch pertains to either the highness or lowness of the tone of the voice. The low-pitched voice most often represents authority and credibility. The high-pitched voice sounds like a small child. If you want to possess vocal power, it is best to practice yourself speaking in a low-pitched voice. The last type of vocalic is rhythm. Rhythmical paces exist in various languages because of the accents. Much like the rest of the vocalic types, rhythm also affects how individuals interact with one another.

Chapter 4: Analyzing Behavioral Patterns

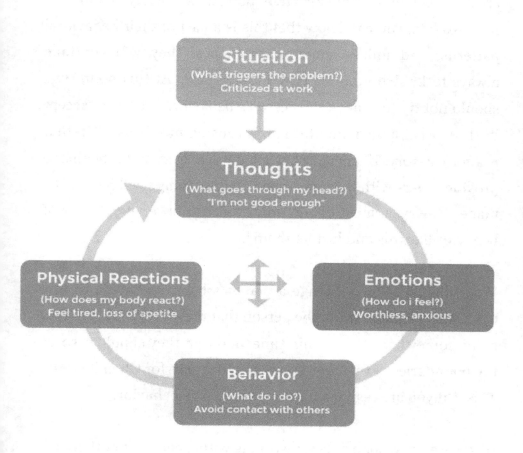

It can be very difficult to understand why people do the things they do. They might be driven by unconscious drives, or they might be hiding their behavior form the world. It is always impossible to know what a person is doing behind the scenes.

This is why it is very important to stick to what is observable about a person's behavior. If a person is usually about five minutes late, you can know that this is a part of their behavioral patterns, and unless something changes, they will continue always to be five minutes late to everything. At this point, you should not try to change the person's behavior, but rather accept it. If their being five minutes late is causing problems, then that is another story. If a person has a habit like this, and it begins to provide others with inconvenience, then a change will have to be made. However, most of the time, you can observe patterns of behavior like this and just let them be.

What does it take to change a person's behavior? Well, in this case, you can just remind the person that they have committed to being somewhere at a certain time, and that they should respect the boundaries of their work item and be there for when it starts. This is if you are responsible for the person's behavior.

If you are not responsible for working with a person, or otherwise have no reason to try to change the behavior, then all patterns must be accepted. This is hard for some people. Some people want everything to work out and be good for them, and they don't know who to accept the world around them.

Acceptance is key here. Accepting behaviors means that you don't judge whatever a person is doing. You can know that their behavior is self-destructive or bad for others, but this doesn't mean that you can't accept their behavior. Acceptance does not mean condoning. What it does mean is that you realize the extent to which you can affect someone else's behavior, and it is really looking at the patterns, which are observable and drawing conclusions from there.

Patterns are observable only in one way to us. It is important not to make assumptions about a person based on their observable behavior patterns. Patterns are merely the data that you have about a person. For example, a person might drink a cup of coffee every morning. Let talk about how much we can surmise just from this one single behavior pattern. One is the aspect of addiction. We can know that this person, judging from this one behavioral trait, has the capacity to be addicted to something. Pretty much all of us do. You cannot, for example, judge that this person is an addict and can't keep themselves from doing this. But a cup of coffee in the morning is an addiction.

Patterns can give your insight into the motivations of a person. If Sarah usually ends up having out with Mark rather than Jessica, this could be from multiple factors. It could be that Mark is a love attraction for her and that her drive to be in a romantic relationship is more important to her right now than her drive for friendships.

Concentration and attention are important skills to have when you are learning to read people. Your attention and concentration must be firmly affixed to one person in order to read them effectively.

People can be read because people's lives are a story. People go thought individualistic things that make them unique and themselves. Each person has a life story with many chapters, and each person contains multitudes. It is not a question of if you are able to read people, because people will show themselves to you. It is the question of if you will be able to read them and use that knowledge for your own good.

When you are trying to read another person, try to focus all of your attention on them, but still while observing them in a neutral way. Check out their posture. Are they standing up straight? Are they crouched or leaning to one side? This can tell you about the physical state of their body. Older people often lean into their posture and will be a bit more hunched over. This is a sign of age. Sitting up straight is a signal that a person is relatively healthy and young.

When people walk, they tend to lead with a certain part of the body. Some people lead with their heads, some lead itch their feet, some lead with the chest. This can give you great insight into the person's drives and how they conduct themselves. A person who leads with the chest may be proud and strong, and they like their physical appearance. If a man has shrugged shoulders that hang down and leads more with the waist, this gives you the idea that they are carefree and laid back. If a woman leads with her hips, it means that she is feeling confident. There are all kinds of ways that body language can give your insight into a person's personality.

One of them is how touchy or physically affectionate a person is. Some people like to have hugs the entire life, and they life to connect physically on a basic level in everyday life and conversation. Other people are not so comfortable with physical contact and prefer to eschew hugs for handshakes and a nod of the head. Neither of these is correct, as there is no correct approach to this. You just have to be cognizant of the boundaries that exist, i.e., not hugging a person who clearly doesn't want the physical contact.

The next main point to consider when you are reading people is the effect. What do we mean by effect? The effect is the way that the face is expressing thoughts and feelings. A normal effect is considered one that has a wide range of expression, for example, smiling when one is happy and having facial expressions that match what one is saying and doing. The effect is a big clue to how someone is feeling. People with some mental illness, for example, have flat affects. This means that their effect does not change very much when they say different things, and they're not able to express feelings with their faces. This comes with a variety of conditions. However, much less severe cases of restricted affect can come simply from being shy, anxious, or sad. A person may restrict their effect when they have social anxiety, for example. A person's thoughts can be wildly swinging all over the place, and their face is displaying a neutral, calm reaction. This can be a protective mechanism for some people, for when you hide your emotions; you and other people don't have to deal with the messy reality of where your emotions are. Some people display all of their feelings their face. When speed-reading people, you just have to determine who much a person's effect is actually representing their feelings. Then, you can engage.

Eye contact is a huge part of this. How much eye contact is the person making? Is it sustained and intimate? Is it broken up? Sometimes, people can be aggressive with eye contact, and it can actually be a way for people to act out their dominance in a situation.

Eye contact is a proximal thing that can connect and divide people. The term Male gaze" was coined to describe the interaction in eye contact or gaze alone. The male gaze is what it is because of the power of the eye. It is something that we often forget, but eye contact is a powerful tool when you make eye contact with someone, you are making a connection. This connection might frighten some people, and people who are shy or have problems with self-esteem will often avoid eye contact to a high degree. This eye contact is causing this a primal level of connection that they do not trust because they don't trust themselves, and they don't have confidence. A person with confidence is able to make eye contact with anyone they encounter and engage with them. People might be intimidating, but you can always engage with someone in good faith and have confidence in yourself to represent yourself and your ideas effectively.

The only way to start reading people is by practicing. You can give yourself some practice by intentionally putting yourself in a situation where you will be around other people and trying to observe them. Observe their tiny movements, try to see how they hold themselves by looking into their eyes. Do not try to linger, just try to make the interaction as normal as possible, with observing as much as you can about the person.

When you get home, write about it. Try to recreate whatever you saw and observed in the person and try to get every little detail known onto the paper. Try to describe what you saw in that person's emotional state, their effect, their smile or lack thereof, their body language, what words they used, and everything else.

Chapter 5: How to Overcome Manipulation

Reasons we allow ourselves to be manipulated

The only time when manipulation is considered successful is the time when you allow it to control your emotions and thoughts. Thus, you must start to distinguish what is going on in you that allows you to be easily manipulated by other people. The three most basic reasons we let ourselves to be manipulated are as follows:

- **Fear**

This emotion comes in numerous structures. We, as human beings, tend to fear losing a relationship; we may fear the disapprobation of other people; we dread to make somebody discontent with our actions. We additionally dread the dangers and outcomes of the manipulator's actions. Imagine a scenario in which they really prevail at doing what they threaten.

- **Guilt**

Today, we are clouded by the idea and responsibility that we should dependably prioritize the needs and wants of other people rather than our own. At times when people would talk about the right to fulfill their own needs and wants, manipulators frequently abuse us and endeavor to allow us to feel like we are accomplishing something immoral in the event that we do not generally put their needs and wants in front of our own. Those individuals who are skilled at these manipulative tactics would tend to define love as the act of fulfilling their needs and wants as part of your obligation. Hence, in the event that we have an opinion that goes against their beliefs, we are manipulated into thinking that we are heartless; at this point, they would make us feel very regretful of our existence and would use guilt to manipulate us.

• **Being too nice**

We appreciate being a provider, fulfilling individuals, and dealing with the needs of other people. We discover fulfillment. Moreover, our confidence would regularly originate from doing what we can for other people. In any case, at times when there is lack of an unmistakable feeling of these and fair limitations, skilled manipulators are able to detect this in people who are easy targets of this phenomenon, and will use certain tactics to further their own selfish gains.

What you need to do to overcome manipulation

We have come to a point where we are here to talk about the basic skills to overcome manipulation. Over the past chapters, we have stressed the fact that manipulation is only successful if the one being manipulated is unaware of the manipulative acts being performed by the manipulator. Moreover, manipulation would only work if you allow them to control you. Much like hypnosis, any hypnosis is actually self-hypnosis. What we are trying to state here is that knowledge that you are being manipulated defeats its entire purpose. For this section of the last chapter of this book, we will discuss some of the most important techniques to overcome manipulation, which is as follows:

• **Establish a clear sense of self**

There is a need to know your identity, what your needs and wants are, what your emotions are, and what you are fond of and not fond of. You must learn to accept these and not become apologetic, as these are the things that make you. At times, we dread that in the event of speaking up, we are viewed by others as egotistical and called out for being selfish. Nevertheless, knowing your identity or what you really need in life is not at all an act of selfishness. Self-centeredness is demanding that you always get what you want or that other has always put your needs and wants first. Similarly, when another person calls you out for not following their orders or fulfilling their needs and wants, they are the ones being selfish, not you.

• Say "no" despite the other person's disapproval

The ability to say "no" despite somebody's objection is a solid demonstration. Individuals who can do this are present in reality. Because in reality, there is no way that we can accommodate all of their needs and wants. When this happens, they will become baffled, even disappointed. However, keep in mind that what they are feeling is part of human nature. Most of these individuals would then forgive and forget. Sound individuals realize that getting what you want all the time is not possible, even when the desires are genuine. In any case, when we cannot endure another person's mistake or objection, it really ends up hard stating "no." It winds up more diligently for us to state it or have limits. Manipulators exploit this shortcoming and use dissatisfaction and objection in extraordinary structures to get us to do what they need.

• Tolerate the other person's negative affect

We can demonstrate compassion for people's pity, hurt, or even annoyance when accommodating them without having the need to back down and reverse our decision. Keep in mind, a solid relationship is described by common minding, shared genuineness, and shared regard. In the event that you are involved with somebody who uses manipulation and unhealthy control consistently, begin to see little propensities that may not be clear to you at first. As you are more grounded, you are better ready to endure how the other individual's negative impact on you is only bringing you down. Thus, this turns into a positive development that liberates you from their manipulative grasps. This will engender a complexity of sorts with the people in your life. It is possible that the manipulator will start to withdraw and consider your time, your emotions, your wants, and your needs, or they will proceed onward to someone else who is an easy target of manipulation practices.

Basic tricks used by manipulators

As soon as you have realized how knowledge of certain truths about yourself can enlighten you to notice manipulative tactics by other people, you will start to divulge from what you are to what a manipulator can do. With that in mind, if you wish to overcome manipulation, you need to be wary of the basic tactics used by manipulators. Once you have a firm grasp as to what you want and what you do not want, you can go head-to-head with a manipulator and even counter some of their most-used techniques. Nevertheless, always keep in mind that as soon as you realize that you are being manipulated, the manipulator loses. It is simply a matter of whether or not you wish to turn the tables and become the manipulator yourself.

• Accusing your rival of what he is blaming you for

This is often referred to as the act of pointing to another person's wrongdoing. When enduring an onslaught and experiencing difficulty regarding safeguarding themselves, manipulators tend to reverse the situation. They blame their rival for committing the exact things that they are being blamed for. *"You state that I don't love you! I think it is you who does not cherish me!"*

• Appealing to power

Numerous individuals are in wonderment of those in power or authority, or those who have status. What's more intriguing is that there are various images to which individuals experience extraordinary dedication. Remember, those who are easily manipulated admire those who are in power. Moreover, those who are in power are aware of their ability to control others by never criticizing them. Instead, they use complex misleading tactics to maneuver their thoughts and alter their decision-making process.

Rabble-rousers that effectively control individuals realize that the vast majority are promptly deceived along with these statements. As a result, they collaborate themselves with those in power. This entails the need to look for experts and other educated individuals that will support their perspectives or, at least, not criticize them.

Cigarette organizations once enlisted researchers who were arranged to state that there is not any confirmation that these products can cause lung disease; however, they knew that the proof was already there. Cigarette organizations additionally established The American Tobacco Foundation, a group of specialists trying to find the impacts of smoking on a person's wellbeing. However, in all actuality, the analysts were actually trying to shield the interests of the tobacco business under the pretense of a logical idea that smoking is not dangerous. They misled the public beguiling them into believing that they were speaking logically precautionary measures.

• Appealing to encounter

Gifted manipulators and con artists, as well as politicians, would often state that they already have experienced or encountered certain situations in their life, which makes them someone who is in power, which can be associated with the previous point. Nevertheless, this appeal to experience provides them with an image of someone who is capable; this may be used to attack their opponent's lack of experience, even though they themselves have experiences that are limited. You can easily identify this manipulation tactic at times when someone is trying to distort their capabilities about a particular subject.

• Appealing to fear

People have fears. The unscrupulous manipulators realize a reality that individuals will, in general, respond crudely when any of these feelings of dread are enacted. Subsequently, they speak to themselves as being able to ensure individuals against these dangers, even when they are not capable of doing so. This is the same for when we talked about giving the target a glimpse of how their most desired outcome is achievable, without really providing it to them. Nonetheless, there are politicians and legislators who frequently utilize this methodology to ensure that individuals line up behind administrative experts and do what the legislature – that is, the thing that the government officials – need.

• Appealing to sympathy

Manipulators are able to depict themselves and their circumstance to the public in a means to make them feel frustrated about their current situation.

Consider the understudy who, when gone up against the fact that she has not gotten her work done, whimpers, and says, "You don't see how hard my life is. I have so many things to do. It is extremely difficult for me to complete my schoolwork. I am not fortunate like some of my classmates. Since my folks cannot afford to send me to school, I need to work 30 hours every week to pay my own specific manner. When I get back home from work, my flatmate plays music until late at night, so it is difficult for me to get a good night's sleep. What am I expected to do? Offer me a reprieve!"

Utilization of this ploy empowers the manipulator to occupy consideration from those individuals who may be going through the same thing. Nevertheless, appealing to sympathy is a tactic that most politicians would use to redirect the attention of the public to matters that do not affect their demise.

• Appealing to well-known interests

Manipulators and tricksters are always mindful as to how they introduce themselves as persons who possess the right qualities and perspectives among the group of spectators, particularly, the sacred beliefs of the crowd. Everybody has a few partialities, and a great many people feel contempt toward a person or thing. Experts manipulators tend to stir up contempt and prejudices among the crowd.

They suggest that they concur with the group of spectators. They go about as though they have shared ideologies. They attempt to persuade the group of spectators that their enemy does not regard sacred the ideologies that they hold sacred. There is numerous potential in this technique. A particular technique named as the "Just Plain Folks Fallacy" is when an individual infers something along the lines of:

"It is comforting to be back in my home, and with people I can truly trust. It's incredible to be with those who face things squarely; those who utilize their presence of mind to achieve things; individuals who don't have confidence in highfalutin methods for thinking and acting."

• Appealing to confidence

This technique is firmly identified with the past points; yet, it stresses what appears to have breezed through the trial of time.

Individuals are regularly oppressed by the social traditions and standards of their way of life, just as social conventions. What is conventional to most tend to appear as if it is the correct decision? It is important to note that manipulators infer how they regard sacred the ideologies and beliefs that the group of spectators is familiar with. These individuals suggest that their enemy aims to obliterate the customs, as well as social conventions. Moreover, they do not stress over whether or not these conventions hurt guiltless individuals. They make the presence of being autonomous in the crowd's perspectives; yet, it would typically be the exact opposite thing. There is a realization that individuals are generally suspicious of the individuals who conflict with present social standards and built up conventions. They realize enough to stay away from these. As a result, there is a kind of restriction on how social traditions are unwittingly and carelessly bound.

• **Begging the inquiry**

One simple approach to demonstrate a point is to accept it in any case. Think about this model:

"Well, what type of government do you want, a government by liberal do-gooders that is able to shell out your hard-earned dollars or a government controlled by business minds that knows how to live within a strict budget and generate jobs that put people to work?"

The previously mentioned statement incorporates the accompanying suppositions that ought not to be underestimated that (1) a liberal government would burn through cash incautiously and that (2) agents realize how to live inside a limited spending plan and produce occupations that set individuals to work.

One minor departure from this error has been classified as "question-begging epithets," the utilization of expressions is actually a prejudgment of an issue by the manner in which it is allowed. In an instance, "Shall we defend freedom and democracy or cave into terrorism and tyranny?" Through the inquiry along these lines, we abstain from discussing awkward inquiries like: "Yet, would we say we are truly propelling human opportunity? Are we truly democratic or simply expanding our capacity, our control, our predominance, our access to foreign markets?" Keep in mind that the statements individuals utilize when bringing about the truth concerning an issue. There is the regular choosing of statements that surmise the accuracy of the situation on the particular issue.

• Creating a false dilemma

A genuine problem happens when we are compelled to pick between two similarly unsuitable choices. A false dilemma happens when we are convinced that we have just two, similarly inadmissible decisions, when we truly have multiple potential outcomes accessible to us. Think about the accompanying case: *"Either we will lose the war on terrorism, or we should surrender a portion of our traditional freedoms and rights."*

Individuals are frequently prepared to acknowledge a false dilemma since few are agreeable with the complex qualifications. Clearing absolutes is actually a part of their manipulative tactics. There is a need to have clear and basic decisions.

• Hedging what you state

Manipulators frequently hole up behind words, declining to submit themselves or give straightforward replies or answers. This enables them to withdraw at times of need. Whenever they are found forgetting data significant to the current situation, they would think of some other reason for not being able to come up with said information. At the end of the day, when forced, they may be able to give in; however, to be an excellent manipulator, you should renege on your missteps, conceal your mistakes, and gate keep what you state at whatever point conceivable.

• Oversimplifying the issue

Since most people are uncomfortable at comprehending profound or unobtrusive contentions, there are those who are fond of oversimplifying the issue to further their potential benefit. *"I couldn't care less what the measurements inform us*

49

concerning the purported abuse of detainees; the main problem is whether we will be tough on crime. Spare your compassion toward the criminals' victims, not for the actual criminals." The reality being overlooked is that the maltreatment of criminals is a crime in itself. Tragically, individuals with an over-simple mindset could not care less about criminal conduct that victimizes criminals.

• Raising only complaints

Your adversary is giving valid justifications to acknowledge a contention; however, the truth of the matter is that your mind is made up and nothing can change it. Gifted manipulators would react with objections after objections. As their rivals answer one protest after another, they would proceed again to object and object. The implicit mentality of the manipulator is that "regardless of what my rival says, I will continue to object because nothing else will convince me otherwise."

• Rewriting history

The most noticeably awful acts and outrages tend to vanish from chronicled accounts while false dreams can be made to become facts. This phenomenon is often observed with Patriotic History. The composition of a contorted type of history is supported by the adoration of the nation and regularly defended by the charge of the antagonism. The truth of the matter is that our mind is persistently attempting to re-portray occasions of the past to absolve itself and denounce its spoilers. Chronicled composing frequently goes with the same pattern, particularly in the composition of reading material for schools. In this way, in recounting to an anecdote about what has happened, those who perform manipulative tactics do not hesitate to contort the past in the manners in which they accept they can pull off. As usual, the manipulator is prepared with self-justifying excuses.

• Shifting the burden of proof

This act alludes to when an individual has the obligation to demonstrate some of his declarations. A good example would be the instance that happened inside a court. The examiner possesses the obligation to prove guilt past distrust. Furthermore, the defense should not claim the responsibility of having to prove innocence. Those who are capable of manipulating others do not have the need to assume the weight of evidence for what they attest to. Along these lines, they harness the right tool in shifting the burden of proof to their rivals.

• Talking in vague generalities and statements

It is difficult to refute individuals when they cannot be bound. So, as opposed to concentrating on specifics, those who are capable of manipulating others tend to speak in the most unclear phrases that they can pull off. We have already talked about how certain statements and generalities can put another person in a daze, which makes it easier for them to be manipulated. This misrepresentation is well known with politicians. For instance, *"Overlook what the cowardly liberals say. It's the right time to be tough, to be hard on criminals, to punish terrorists, and be tough on those who disparage our nation."* Manipulators ensure they do not utilize particulars that may make individuals question what they are doing in the first place.

• Telling enormous falsehoods and big lies

Majority of the people are liars, even about the little things; yet, there is still a reluctance to say things other than the truth. In any case, these individuals realize that in the event that you insist on a lit long enough, numerous individuals will trust you – particularly, on the off chance that you have the tools of mass media to broadcast a particular lie.

Every gifted manipulator is centered around what you can get individuals to accept, not on what is valid or false. They realize that the human personality does not normally look for reality; it looks for solace, security, individual affirmation, and personal stake.

Actually, individuals regularly would prefer not to know the reality, particularly, certainties that are agonizing, that uncover their logical inconsistencies and irregularities, and that uncover what they hate about themselves or even their nation.

There are so many manipulators that are exceptionally gifted in telling huge lies and, in this manner, causing those lies to appear valid.

Chapter 6: Understanding the Subconscious Mind

Philosophers have long debated the different realms of the mind. Since ancient times, thinkers have discussed and written about the different parts of the psyche; there are the parts that are dedicated to loving, to thinking about material things, to artisticness, to combativeness. However, to talk about the subconscious, we must talk about Freud. Sigmund Freud was one of the most important psychologists and philosophers in the history of man. He lived around the turn of the 19th century, and it was he who developed the concept of psychoanalysis.

The Subconscious in Psychology

Psychoanalysis is a method of uncovering unconscious material through various methods of applied therapy. By sitting on a couch and talking about whatever arose in the person's mind, Freud would be able to analyze that person's life and unconscious motives. Freud believed that people are driven by deep, instinctual, sexually-centered drives. He believed that our animal nature was a considerable part of our psyche and that what we presented to the world was only a small part of the equation.

Think about an iceberg; there is a part that is visible above the water, and that is the conscious mind. What do we mean by the conscious mind? It is the part of the mind, which is thinking, feeling, and expressing itself at the moment. It is the conscious source of material that is easily accessible. The top of the iceberg is the smallest part of the iceberg, however, and if you dive deeper, you can see that most of the iceberg exists underwater. This is what Freud thought about the proportionality of the human psyche. He thought that most of the human psyche was not at the surface, but rather down below in the depths. Most of the unconscious was down where it was difficult to access, and he thought that people didn't really show their true selves unless they were put in a position where this material could be uncovered.

Freud called the different parts of the psyche the ego, the superego, and the id. The Id is the part of us, which is animal in nature. T is the part of us that wants to have sex, eat, and fight. It is the most primal part of humanity and it is the only part of the psyche, which is within us from the very moment that we are born. It might seem dark and scary, but it is the most natural part of us.

The Ego is the part of the psyche, which is grounded in reality. It is the part, which tells us what is doable and controls our reality orientation. The Ego is the part of us, which "converts" the Id's drives into behavior.

The Super Ego is the moral component of our psyche. The superego is what tells us what is appropriate and moral in any given circumstance and it tells us what we think is okay and what we think is unacceptable.

The Id and the Ego are being engaged when people use Dark Psychology and Dark Persuasion. When a person is using these tactics, they are engaging the subconscious, which partly lives in the id and partly lives in the ego.

The subconscious mind is made up of all the memories and associations that you have, and all the experiences with different people that you have. Have you ever tired a portion of food that you had a particularly bad reaction to, or gotten food poisoning? His happens to many people, and many of them discover that after this experience, they are no longer able to eat that food again, for many years. This is the subconscious at work. If the food in question is carrots, then you will find that the next time you encounter carrots, you will be disgusted at the thought of eating them. You will find them repulsive and unnatural. This is because your subconscious has internalized the experience of discomfort and disgust with that particular food. In reality, you know that the food will be fine in future experiences, but you are not actually able to encounter that food and engage with yourself rationally, because you have integrated that bad experience into your psyche. The subconscious is instinctual and has plenty of animalistic qualities to it.

The subconscious is responsible for the sexual drives, which we have. It is governed by the pleasure principle, which basically states that we are driven by pleasure and that pleasure is the ultimate motivator. This is why advertising works so well when it engages ideas of sexual motivation and other forms of pleasure.

The old saying "sex sells" is ever prescient to this day. Think about the phenomenon of sexual attraction. You might understand consciously that you are married, and happily so, but you will still find yourself wanting to engage in sexual conduct with others, even though you have agreed with your partner to not do so. This is the very essence of the id. It is always present, lurking, and it is the most animalistic pressure. In fact, sexuality is often part of Dark Persuasion tactics. A leader is often very attractive in physicality. This is part of charisma and it is a very effective way to engage in someone's subconscious drives.

Sexuality and other base drives are an important part of dark Persuasion. Since the dawn of time, humans have been subject to manipulation due to sexual urges. Sex and drugs have always been a way to control and manipulate a population.

Memory

Memory is a tricky thing. If two people witness an event, they will both have different accounts of that event. One person might remember it as a situation in which they were victimized. Another person might think of it as an event that was fair to all parties involved. Memory can fade and come back within a lifetime. Think about the earliest memory that you have. Undoubtedly, it will be one of your childhood. Is it a pleasant memory, or an unpleasant one? Sometimes the unpleasant memories are what stick out the most.

The mind has several different types of memory. First of all, there are the classifications of long-term memory and short-term memory. As the names would suggest, long-term memory is when you keep something in your mind for a very long time. Short-term memory is where thoughts or experiences are stored while your brain decides to file them in your long-term memory or to let go of them. Explicit memory is a type of long-term memory that will require conscious thought to bring about. This is what you are using when you try to think of your earliest memory. Implicit memory is something that you don't have to try for. This is riding a bike (if you've already learned to do so). That is something that people say never goes away. It is something that you already know how to do, and you don't have to try to do it. It is also the type of memory you are using when you brush your teeth or walk around.

Your muscles do not have to be directed to do these things, because you already know how to do them. Autobiographical memory is your memory of how your life has progressed. This is something that almost everyone has, and it allows you to build a life story.

Subconscious memory is what you are using when you have a "bad feeling" about something. This is similar to intuition. These are very closely related concepts. Intuition and subconscious memory are when you are integrating memories of the past, but you don't know when or where they are coming from, and you don't exactly know the content of this memory. Many people use this type of memory when they are in situations that are dangerous.

This will be something you can lean on to identify instances when you are being manipulated or persuaded, brainwashed or deceived. FI you can tap into this mysterious system of the subconscious, you will be able to defend yourself. This is no easy task, and it takes a lot of trial and error and it takes experience.

Ten Ways to Train the Subconscious

1. Allow yourself to believe the unbelievable.

In order to change your habits or way of thinking, you must fight back against the impulse to believe that nothing can ever change. This is one thing that often gets people stuck; it is the belief that the way they are now will be the way they are forever. Banish this thought, for it will only leave you undeveloped and will keep you away from self-realization.

2. Give yourself permission to be successful.

Many people have in their subconscious the belief that they can never be as successful as they want. Some people have complexes from growing up poor that tell them that they will never have enough money and that they should always act as though having enough money will never be an option for them. We keep ourselves unsuccessful, as well in other ways. Some people think that they can't be creative, or they can't do a certain type of job. You just have to switch this thinking, and when you find these thoughts arising from your subconscious, you can tell yourself consciously that you are capable; you are able to be successful.

3. Resist others' projections.

We are all subject to the projection of others. Projection is when a person has beliefs or feelings about themselves, and they think that all other people are like them. They start to think that everyone around them is actually matching them in some sort of characteristic or habit. People will put you in a box, and expect you to act a certain way. You must allow yourself to totally reject their thoughts about you. Resist their attempts to put you in a box.

4. Give yourself some positive reinforcement.

The very essence of resisting Dark Persuasion is being able to understand the dark forces at work and giving yourself the opposite information. Being able to understand Dark Psychology means that you will have to engage in the darkness just a little bit. However, once you do this, you will have to balance out your energy with some positive thinking as well. If you are able to give yourself positive messages to balance out the negative darkness, you will find that you are able to overcome all manipulation and deception.

5. Be real about your success.

Don't be humble. Of course, being humble is a virtue, but only up to a point. Being humble will eventually lead to your downfall. You need to stand with Machiavelli on this point, and let yourself be able to praise yourself wholeheartedly. Individualism is one of the main tenets of Western culture, and this means embracing yourself, your needs, and your way of living. Celebrate yourself. Tell yourself that you are the one who deserves success. Be real about what you have already accomplished – chances are, you have accomplished a lot.

6. Envision your future.

Be bold about your future. If you are always envisioning a future that is full of pain and suffering, you will probably be working toward making that real. If you are able to create a future vision for yourself that is one of success and domination, you will be much closer to creating that in reality.

7. Point out your own weaknesses so that you can work on them.

Your subconscious will play tricks on you. Sometimes, it will make you think that you are perfect and have no flaws, when in fact, this is not the case. Most people have one or two areas that they can work on. If you are able to point these out to yourself, you will find that you are able to morph more closely towards self-realization.

8. Embrace gratitude.

Embracing gratitude is all about fostering a healthy self-image, which will help you on your path to self-realization. Some people have damaged their subconscious, and they get bitter and weakened because of past failures. You must learn to resist this urge, and you must find gratitude in the world. This will make your defenses stronger and it will teach you that there are things that are worthy of your pursuit of happiness.

9. Identify what you want, and get it.

Stop messing around and keeping yourself from getting what you want. If you don't know how to get it, then try to learn how to get it. If your goal is a certain career path, then ask someone if you can be his or her apprentice. If it is something you can learn on your own, do your research and start to learn how you can achieve this goal on your own. Read books, the internet, and ask other people about how they have achieved what you want to achieve.

10. Get rid of your attachment to the "how".

The "how" is not important. The "how" is what keeps you from getting what you want and need. This is where judgment comes in. The subconscious will sometimes push you towards judgment, and you will find that if you have a voice that pushes you towards judgment, this will start to create a space between what you want and where you are. You should work to reduce this space as much as possible.

Chapter 7: Charisma and Machiavellian Confidence

Confidence and charisma are ways to both employ dark psychological tactics on others as well as protect yourself from being manipulated by others. What do you think of when you think about confidence?

Rather than focusing on the modern conception of positive psychology's confidence, let's roll back the tape of history a little bit and consider Machiavelli's style of confidence. Machiavellianism is defined as a cold and calculating ability to work for and towards your own goals, for yourself. It does not emphasize morality or empathy, and it is an essentially cynical mindset.

Why cynical? The reason that this approach can be so successful boils down to the animal nature of human beings. Essentially, we are animals who are all trying to protect ourselves. Why? There are a few reasons. Some of us are focused on being able to extend the family line through the creation of the family. There is certainly a biological drive, and some would say a spiritual drive, to do so. Others are merely focused on the legacy of their own life, which is a worthy drive in and of itself.

Nice guys finish last. That's the mindset of Machiavellianism. It is all about strength. Cynicism helps to frame the world in a realistic way. People are out to get you and they want to stop you from accomplishing your goals. Think about it. There are not very many people who are actually just in the world. Justice is a concept that is very fluid, and it rarely is placed on the right people. The world is filled with predators, people who want to take advantage of other people. The world is filled with con artists, scams, businesses, mind control, brainwashing, and darkness.

That is not to say that there is no light in the world as well, but that's not what you have to worry about. You have to worry about being taken advantage of, you have to worry about protecting you and your family from evil. What kinds of evil? There are many kinds of pervasive evil in the world. Some of the kinds are ones that are already listed in this book. There are aloes other kinds, which have not been mentioned.

Machiavellian confidence is all about looking that evil in the face, realizing that it is there for a reason, and refusing to be taken advantage of. It is all about being stronger than the enemy.

First of all, you have to actually be stronger than the enemy, whatever that looks like for you. Physical strength is not everything, but some people feel much better if they put themselves in a place where they can be stronger than most other people. This will give you the upper hand in physical altercations, and it will also set you on a plane of development that will help in your pursuit of confidence. Confidence does not have to come from physical strength, however.

Some of the greatest kings who ever existed were small, wiry, and full of weakness in their physical body. What did they know how to do? They knew how to exercise their power of will. They knew how to motivate people, to get people behind them in their search for power, they knew how to drum up support and get people angry. Physical power can only take you so far. Then, you have to start thinking metaphysically.

Looking Inward

One thing that many people have to face to reach this state of confidence is to address their unfinished business. This is not business in the conventional meaning of the word. This is business in any form, whether it comes from past relationships, things that happened, things that you have been putting off for a while, or many other things. There can be many sources for unfinished business that have to be addressed.

Some people have relationships within their family that have to be addressed. We all didn't just one day appear as adults, we had to go through the process of development that every other human did. That means having a childhood. For many people, this must be addressed in order to reach the heights of confidence that we are talking about. Childhood contains many things: memories, reasons for living, habits formed, and personality created. Many people must look back on their childhood to make sense of what happened in order to find this place of Machiavellian confidence. Perhaps you were made to think that you have to always follow the rules when you were a child. This is how many people raise their children They raise them to think that you always have to fear and respect your elders, that you must bend your will to authority, and that you are not worthy of being an authority yourself. If this was how you were raised, you will have to address those experiences and push back against them. You must able to tell yourself that you are worthy of being an authority yourself, that you have the skill, power, and worth to be an authority in this world. You must tell that little child version of yourself that it's okay, you were told wrong, and now you are going to be powerful. On the other hand, if you were spoiled as a child, and told that you are already powerful and that you already have a fear of authority, even when you had not earned it, this will be something that you will have to learn as well. Confidence doesn't come from an unfounded place. You must learn to be humbled once or twice to actually earn what is called Machiavellian confidence. You can't learn this without failing a few times. Failure is what will show you your limits. When you are shown your limits, then you must go back and redefine them.

Unfinished business might be a romantic situation in which you felt that you were left in the lurch. Go back, do some writing and personal investigation, and see what you can find in that situation to make yourself integrate the experiences. Life is all about putting together the pieces of the puzzle that is your past. Once you put together the pieces of the puzzle, you'll be able to be yourself to higher consciousness.

Unfinished business can be based in habits that you already have. One of the most common is addiction. Addiction can be too many things. Sometimes it is drugs, sometimes it is alcohol, sometimes it is just thinking.

Many people develop an addiction to drugs in order to fill some void that they have in their thinking or other parts of their life.

Drugs are often a way to make up for a loss of confidence or a lack of other strength characteristics.

An addict has two elements: dependence and denial. The dependence comes from some lack that exists in their lives. The denial is the lack of strength to know what you are addicted to something. The dependence usually comes from a place of missing something. This could be love, it could be confidence, and it could be a closeness with others. The lack usually has something to do with childhood, and it is something that people often don't understand until they are able to process their lives later on. The addict gets into the habit of learning that they can cope with the world in this particular way.

For example, if there is a young man who grows up and goes to college and starts drinking right away in college that is probably because he does not have the people skills or confidence to interact with others. When he was younger, he did not learn what it is like to be able to interact with other people and make friends without drinking. So, when he gets to college, he feels lost. He doesn't feel like h knows how to be himself when he is around other people he might feel that he is weird or uninteresting to the people. Whatever it is, it means that he doesn't fit in. It means that he feels that there is not a place for him. The effects of alcohol will ease this. Alcohol gives him a purpose. It greases the gears of social interaction and it lets him feel like he is able to be himself, to be loud, be confident, and express himself with whatever he wants to say.

You can see how there is a void here that has been filled with the drug experience. No matter how much you try and fill the void with that drug, it won't be fulfilled until you go back and figure out why you are missing something. That is what is known as unfinished business.

Unfinished business will keep you from being yourself. It will keep you from achieving the levels of confidence that are possible for all people. You must go back, learn, and work to achieve understanding for your past condition in order to be able to achieve the type of Machiavellian confidence that we are talking about.

Self-Realization

Self-realization is a term that comes from the humanistic school of psychology. It is a term that references the idea that each person has an authentic self inside somewhere that can be reached through the process of understanding the self and doing work to achieve a more authentic and real you.

Humanistic psychology posits that when we are born, we start to absorb whatever is around us like a sponge. We start to learn behaviors. At first, we are an essence. We are just ourselves. It is a heady concept to think about: that when you are born, you are purely yourself, nothing else, and as you go on, you start to learn personality traits and learned behaviors. As this progresses, you get further and further away from yourself. This is not necessarily true; there could be a parental system that helps very young people to be very authentic in their entire lives. However, most of us were raised by imperfect parents, and at a certain point, we learned how to cope with the world in ways that took us away from our natural selves. This is a hypothesis that is not necessarily true across the board, but it is a useful way of thinking to be able to understand the construct of the authentic self and self-realization. Self-realization is also influenced by Maslow's pyramid of needs.

The pyramid of needs is a system that describes what is the most necessary and needed parts of life. It stars with food, shelter, and the very basic necessities of life. Then, it moves into more extraneous parts of life, like work and fulfillment. At the top of the triangle is self-realization. How does this relate to Dark Persuasion and Machiavellian confidence?

In order to make it to the top of the pyramid in your life development, you will need to meet all of the previous requirements. This means learning what it is for you to have dependable, meaningful work, a love life, relationships, family, and emotional expression. All of these needs must be met, and if any of them are missing, you will be left with a weakened sense of self. A strong sense of self is what gives people the strength to go on in the world and make sense of things. People who are missing the lower parts of the triangle will find that they are more prone to being manipulated.

If we take this to the most literal level, imagine if you are starving. You live in a place where there is very little food, and it is work just to be able to eat every day. Imagine someone comes along and says that if you join their religion or club, you will be fed every day. Of course, you will join their club, because you need food. The other parts don't matter. You don't really have a good choice here; the best choice is to join up and do whatever is required of you to be a part of the club so that you are able to get food and water every day.

This is true for the rest of the pyramid as well. This happens to people who are lacking a family system. If you don't have a family system, you are not able to feel secure in the world. This makes people more susceptible to joining cults and other organizations that take advantage of people. Cults often prey on the weak and lonely, and they offer up a place to have family and a place where they can find support in their lives, rather than being alone. The cult uses this as a manipulation tactic to make the person think a certain way. After the cult has gained enough followers, they are able to have power. Each person adds to the leader's power. The reason that people are recruited is that they are missing one of the levels of the pyramid of needs. Each person needs a family and a system of support, and if they don't have that, they are more easily manipulated.

So, in the grand scheme of things, you should always be working towards self-realization. This will ensure that you have a life path that is working toward your own health and success.

Communication

Let's talk for a moment about communication. Communication is a huge part of being an effective leader, and it is very important if you want to have charisma and confidence. We use words to describe things, people, feelings, attitudes, theories, philosophies, and so on. We can choose many different words to describe the same thing- and this is where the trouble often starts. Let's say the foreman says that the shop assistant made an unfortunate decision. The union members in the shop assume he means that the assistant made the wrong decision. It is quite obvious to them that the foreman is being unfair by criticizing the assistant. The foreman counters by saying that it would be best if the men just forget the whole matter.

"Forget it" is something you say to someone when you get fed up with their inability to see and accept your point of view. It is often the same as saying "I can't get through to you. You're either too stupid or too stubborn to see the truth." Yet the foreman may simply have been expressing his desire to escape from an unexpected conflict. The whole problem here was the failure by both sides to correctly interpret the relationship between the words and the reality.

Man has advanced through the use of language, but for the same reason, the complexity of human language has created many of his problems. There would be less misunderstanding if each object and feeling had only one single word to describe it. This is not the case and is suspect that we are rather glad that that is not the case. However, recognition and acceptance of this verbal communication problem is the first step in overcoming it.

Each person, object, or idea can be described by many different words, and each word might well trigger a unique response from every person to whom it is directed. This process is easy to understand if we can accept the idea of the human mind being much like a computer. Information can be fed into a computer and stored there for future reference. The human mind works the same way. The mind is the storehouse of information and attitudes which are stockpiled there as the result of all past experiences.

Much of the information stored in the human mind may never be used; the conscious mind may not even be aware of the existence of some of the information kept in the dark recesses of the subconscious, but nevertheless, it is there. When you hear the word Siberia, what comes into your mind? Bitter cold? Desolation? Chances are good that you have never actually been to Siberia, but past experiences – what you have read, heard, and seen in pictures- have been stored in your mental computer. The word Siberia is fed into that computer and you respond with a mental image of the place called Siberia which is distinctly your own and may be quite unlike that of another person.

Our failure to recognize the arbitrary relationship between the word and the object (that the word is not the thing) is made clear at one point in the novel Bread and Wine by Ignazio Silone. There is a scene in the book involving some men playing a card game called the settemezzo. In this game, the kind of diamonds is the key card and their particular kind of diamonds is worn out from handling and is easily recognizable. One of the players suggests substituting the three of spades for the card. A heated discussion erupts because of the players' claims such a substitution would be impossible. He flatly says: "The king of diamonds is always the king of diamonds. He may be filthy, torn, or have holes in him, but he's still the king of diamonds.

We also make the mistake of thinking that words can give us certain guarantees. We assume that fine-sounding word guarantees quality. You think not? If you were to drive into a strange town while on a trip, and stopping for lunch, you noticed there were but two restaurants in town, which one would you choose: Mom's Place or Ptomaine Corners? Chances are, you would choose Mom's Place, simply because the name seems to give you a certain guarantee.

This brings us to the definitions of connotation and denotation. The sharpest denotation would be the thing itself, the object. Since we are speaking of language, we must apply denotation to the world of words and infer that denotation is the factual language we use to describe something. Denotation is best exemplified by the dictionary definition. It is the connotative language that we are most interested in because it is the language we most often use.

In order to become the type of person who is able to use their Machiavellian confidence, you must be a person who understands this material and is able to use it for your advantage. A person with Machiavellian confidence knows how to communicate. Think about how much communication has evolved in the past couple of decades. Rather than spending time writing out books and papers as previous generations did, younger people these days have less impetus than ever to engage their writing skills and actually create something that is of value. Gone, too, is the power of verbal communication. FI you visited universities in the 1970s and '80s and had conversations with the students, you would notice a marked difference from the communication skills that are presented in students today. It is just a fact that social media has greatly reduced people's capacity for strong verbal communication.

So, you, as a Machiavellian, should be able to master this realm of communication. When you say something, you should say it clearly and directly. Say what you mean the way you want to be perceived. You cannot be afraid to express yourself. This is what confidence is all about: expressing yourself. If you have fear about expressing yourself, you should look deeper into that fear and see where it is emanating from. Is it that you are afraid of being judged?

If it is the fear of being judged, you have to address this. Nobody's judgment can be put above your own. You must be your own god in the world. You must place your judgment above everyone else's in the entire world.

You Are What You Think

Ever heard the expression, "you are what you eat"? There is a variation on that phrase that I enjoy it goes: "You are what you think". When you think negative thoughts about yourself, you are participating in a sort of self-loathing self-fulfilling prophecy. If you are always telling yourself that you are lazy and worthless, you encourage yourself to do types of behaviors that you consider worthless or lazy. You start to think about yourself as the worst version of yourself. This is something that needs to be battled against. Positive thinking is much better for your overall health. Positive thinking will improve hour mood and attention span and even your physical health.

IT starts with a perspective change. You must think about yourself, what do I criticize about myself? Why do I criticize myself? You've gone to first identify the ways in which you bring yourself down. This may be an easier process for some than others. Some people have body issues. They don't like the way they look, or they find that they are continually putting themselves and possibly others down for their looks in its extreme, this is known as body dysmorphic disorder. This type of person will need to learn how to do two things: The first is to decide what they want to do, and are actually capable of doing, about their looks. This could be a practice of starting to jog or some other form of exercise. It could involve eating better.

Whatever goes down, it just has to be something attainable and gentle. The second task is to let go of whatever you are holding that is negative about your appearance. You can just let that go and say, "I've been exercising lately, which is something that I can do to improve my appearance. That is enough work for me to do in this area." and forgive the rest. You've got to face that voice that is telling you to look horrible and disgusting because that voice is essentially just you. Sometimes we have bullies or abusive people in your lives, and they tell us to mean things about ourselves. Often, though it is coming from our own consciousness.

Positive thinking means that you are shifting from the perspective of bleakness and gloominess and starting to acknowledge the beautiful things that you do experience often times, it is o that there aren't beautiful experiences in our lives, but rather than we are not accessing the experiences that are right in front of us. Positive thinking means shifting just a little, fro "ugh, its dark out today and I don't want to go to work" to "its dark out today, but I am going to do my best at work and maybe take a nap afterward." It is not all sunshine and rainbows. The positive thing should be realistic and attainable.

Confidence will be greatly strengthened when you get into positive thinking. Confidence is something that is difficult to measure and difficult to grow. It comes from deep down in the spirit, and it knows that one can be kept safe and sound by his or her own will. Confidence comes from self-security. If there are a bunch of things that you hold in shame, like past experiences, or other sources of embarrassment, you will not find it easy to have confidence. To have confidence, you must let all that stuff go and admit to yourself that you are a person who is worthy of being listened to, hear, and understood, and then communicate yourself that way.

The best and most classic way to be confident is to be yourself and to own it. If you are a tall person, love that you are tall and share it with the world. If you are a short person, own it and love your shortness. There are all kinds of body traits and all kinds of people who love people with your body traits. Whatever mental or physical traits you might have insecurities about, you just have to give up on those anxieties and let go. This will better you in the long run. Motivation is extremely important to address for people with depression. Depression in large part very dependent on motivation. The lack of motivation is what drives depression, and often times this turns into a cycle of lack of motivation and negative feelings. Motivation is a nebulous concept, but we can pretty much say with confidence that when your body is healthier, you are generally more motivated. When you are spending all of your time on addiction or in unhealthy habits, you are feeding this cycle and your motivation will be cut short. This is unfortunate, but it happens.

A big part of positive thinking is learning to self-talk about good things and also to separate yourself from the bad thoughts. You can just let yourself know that thoughts are not real. You don't have to disprove thoughts, you can just say that they are mean or unnecessary and do away with them. Lots of people out there pace way to much value on their thoughts, their tiny little thoughts, and their content, and they spend all of their time "strategically" thinking, as to bring out some kind of satisfaction. But the satisfaction never comes.

What is helpful for this situation is to learn how to tell yourself declarations. You are not your thoughts. Your thoughts only exist in your head. Sometimes they are correct, or true, and sometimes they are not. It doesn't matter. In either case, they do not make you up. You are not a good person or a bad person for what you think.

Chapter 8: Detach from Emotions

When tapping into Dark Psychology and its uses, it is important to pay attention to the role that emotion is playing in your decisions. Many of our important decisions will undoubtedly be imbued with emotion. Some of them are relatively easy; others take a great deal of learning and getting through challenges. Often times, we will need to detach from emotions. This chapter is about the situations that drive this need and some strategies to be healthily detached from emotions. Emotions are useful for some things, obviously. They can help you to gain motivation, and feeling joy and pride is one of the rewards for living a good life. Emotions are a necessary and ever-present thing. However, you must learn to separate from these experiences and know that they are not necessarily real. It might be hard to tear yourself away from feeling sad. You might not be able to at all. However, you must learn just to let that experience be. You can't let it take over your entire day. You have to let yourself let go of the "importance" of that emotion.

People who are driven only by emotions are carried away in whatever is happening. They are not able to use the logical side of their brain, rather letting their sadness happiness, joy, or depression take them away somewhere else.

First of all, let's talk about what we're not talking about. When talking about detaching from emotions, we are not talking about becoming cold and disconnected. This can be a source of coping for some people; they become disconnected and "detached" from emotions and use this to be unhealthy and justify it in their minds. This can be described as being aloof. These people are afraid of intimacy and connection. They are afraid of engaging with the world on an emotional level. Of course, we are emotional creatures, and emotions will always be a part of our experience as human beings. We cannot part with this aspect of humanity, thank God. We have to learn to live with our emotions and use them in appropriate ways.

True detachment leads not to disconnection and aloofness, but rather to an ability to be wise. Wisdom is described as the ability to use knowledge. Well, detachment helps along the process of wisdom. We cannot use our knowledge if we rely too much on the emotional information that we are experiencing to make a decision. In order to use the knowledge, we have to make decisions and understand our world, we have to contextualize our emotions. Wisdom comes from this contextualization. True detachment involves acknowledging our emotional states and dealing with them in the most efficient manner. When we are detached from emotion, we are able still to engage in emotion while not letting it take over our decision-making.

We've mostly all heard this one before: "when you assume, you make an Ass out of U and Me." this is an important lesson, and understanding ours and other's biases is a big part of not assuming. As we discussed in the last chapter, understanding biases can help you to realize when you are unfairly assuming something about another person or situation.

The first things to ask yourself when you are thinking about the reason you assume things are this: Are you a psychic? Do you have a crystal ball that tells the past, future, and present truth? I bet not! You may be a psychic with these powers, and if you are, you should disregard this chapter. For the rest of us, it takes to realize that we are not omniscience and that we can't tell what is going on in other people's minds.

We tend to think of more attractive people as more trustworthy. There are scientific studies that show that people tend to have a bias and assume that people who are physically good-looking have good personality traits, more than we would assume for people who are less traditionally good-looking. Why is this? On its face, it seems totally shallow and ridiculous. There is an explanation, however, for this tendency, if we look to evolutionary theory. People used to choose partners based on physical traits that they felt would ensure their survival. So, it follows that men who were the strongest and fastest would find mates and women who were determined the most physically adapted to take care of children and keep the family functional would be chosen. In men, this led to the propagation of certain traits, and a selectiveness for men who are physically tall, powerful, and muscular. For women, this developed into an idealized mate who had a body that appeared fertile and "womanly." However, we are past that now. We no longer need to choose mates that will defend us from the megafauna of the past. We don't need to choose in this way anymore, but we still have vestiges from the past embedded in our psychology. This has resulted in the expectations of gender that we have inculcated in our population.

Another idea to consider is this: you have no idea what another person is going through. Pain and suffering are subjective. Some people hide their pain from the world. They may present as a happy-go-lucky, content person, but really, they have hip arthritis that makes it hard to walk. People may be hiding emotional pain in just the same ways.

We can't assume that we know that people are going through our how they are feeling internally. Sometimes, we will misinterpret a smile or facial expression. If you have some ideas about a person like if they are mad at you, you may see the smallest physical move, as a move of aggression, or you might find that you interpret their speech too hastily for anger.

How do you stop assuming things? You should analyze your thoughts and see when you are assuming and then try to get to the why of assuming. Why are you doing these things? Sometimes, people start the critical thinking process without having all the facets. They may fill in the information into the process that is untrue; to draw conclusions before they can actually be drawn. You can pay attention to how much our mind is doing this; they try to redirect when you are noticing the assumptions. You might find that you have some biases that you had now acknowledged before.

There are three ways of thinking to consider when you are analyzing your thinking. The first is the emotional mind. This mind makes decisions under duress and will be only taking into account the data that is coming from the emotions. The emotional mind will be frenzied, whirling, and unstoppable. It will be passionate and driven by love, art, humor, and romanticism. The next way of thinking is the logical mind. The logical mind is driven to make decisions without any source of emotional data whatsoever. The logical mind can ignore a crying face. It can deny emotion and prove to the world that it has never felt anything, ever. It was a way to self-denial that can be very satisfying for some people. Most people don't make decisions this way, but some do. The logical mind is not good at understanding people in a whole way; it totally relies on scientific observations and quantifiable data. The third, more moderate way of thinking is the wise mind. The wise mind takes into account both the emotional mind and the logical mind when it is making decisions. It addresses the problems of emotionality and the problems of logic. It takes input from both of their perspectives; if the emotional mind is saying something, it listens and responds gently. If the logical mind is making its case, it weighs the importance of logic in that situation. The wise mind is a beautiful synthesis of these two forms of human awareness. IT is called the wise mind because it embodies the wisdom that we see in the most intelligent and efficient people. Often, you will find that older people have more wisdom. This is not true for all older adults, but a lot of them. They have acquired more wisdom simply because they have had more practice in making a decision. Over and over again, they have made decisions. Maybe sometimes they had let the emotional mind take over their decisions, and they saw how that played out. They have also witnessed the ravages of the logical mind, a mind that is disconnected and aloof, and seen the effect that that way of thinking has on their decisions. Often, older wise people are known as "not giving a damn." Simply, put, they don' sweat the small stuff. They have a perspective on life that is influenced by having lived through most of it. They know the importance of emotions, but they also know not to get too wrapped up in it.

Let's face it: it's great to live in emotions. It can be a very indulgent thing. Some people can even enjoy the melancholy sadness that comes with depression .it becomes a certain flavor to your file. There is a certain sweetness to depression, and it can be satisfying, especially for artists and creatives, to live in this sadness and relish it. It feels food for them to be sad. It sounds worrying, but that is the way that we adapt to our lives sometimes. Other people may be more comfortable with the emotion of anger; they will find themselves resorting to angry actions or words to get their point across or get things done. These emotions are states that we hold on to because we feel that they will help us somewhat. Outside of normal emotional functioning, however, there exists the other side to the story the logical mind. The logical mind works with reason and practicality. If you find yourself having trouble detaching from emotion, try embracing the logical mind. The logical mind is what you use when you are scheduling things, doing at problems, or planning a trip by calculating gas mileage. It doesn't need any emotional input to make decisions. However, you must remember that the goal is not to become disconnected and aloof, but rather just detached. Healthy detachment is necessary.

Some people will stand in your way when you try to detach from emotion. Some people want to see you wound up, to see you emotional because they want you to continue the patterns of behavior that you have been engaging with before. Change is hard for people to accept. The people who react negatively to someone being more detached from emotion do react negatively because they are bad people, but because they are people with fears, desires, wants, and needs like the rest of us. This hold not, however, stops you from changing your mindset and behavior in order to more thoroughly detach from emotion.

You see, we each have patterns of thinking, feeling, and behavior. Our patterns get interwoven with the people around us. This can happen in positive and negative ways. For example, there may be someone you often see who you like. They say hi to you, you say hi to them, and you feed off of each other/ energy. This is a great way to have an interpersonal relationship – simple, easy, and low pressure. Another way we get intertwined with people is in our intimate relationships. When we are dating or married to someone, we have a different set of ways that we interact with him or her. For one, you may have a sexual relationship with this person. You may be more honest with this person that you are with other people You might find that yon your relationship with them, you are subject to each other's needs, even physical needs, more often than other people are subjected to them. This is fine and good. Sometimes, however, we get used to accommodating our partner or spouse's need too much, and we take on negative behaviors that accompany or complement others' bad habits. Here's an example: Jane has three sisters. They are loud, boisterous, and fun. She is the youngest. As Jane is halfway through high school, she gets her first boyfriend her sisters all give her lots of teasing about it and makes fun of her from "K-I-

S-S-I-N-G" in the tree and all of that. So, this is her first stressor: she feels pressure and anxiety from her sisters, who like to point out a relationship that is new and unknown in her life. Her new boyfriend, Dan, is a sneaky guy. Jane is attracted to Dan's "bad boy" status and often is seen accompanying him on his cigarette breaks outside of school, even though she doesn't smoke. Dan likes that Jane comes with him on his smoke breaks, because he, after all, does feel little unhealthy and ashamed about his habit. So, when Jane starts to be more reluctant about being around Dan when he is smoking, Dan reminds her that "I feel lonely out there, and I don't want to be alone." Jane starts to consistently stay with Dan when he is, and eventually, she picks up the habit for herself. Jane's parents notice her new habit, and they are not happy. They have a long talk with Jane, and they tell her about the risks associated with smoking. They tell her about addiction and about how cigarettes work in the body. Jane understands all this and is convinced that smoking isn't for her. Even though she likes Dan, and wants to be his girlfriend, she doesn't want to smoke. So now Jane has a big problem: first, she has to deal with the teasing of her sisters, but now, she has to deal with the teasing all while starting to modify her behavior. Dan approaches her after lunch on the following Monday and asks her to come outside with him to smoke. Jane decides that she doesn't want to do this anymore, and she tells Dan just that. He starts to go on his diatribe about how lonely and sad it is to be let alone during these times, and Jane starts to feel a little sad for him. She stops, however, and detaches from her emotions. She says to Dan, "I'm sorry that you feel lonely. I have made a personal decision for myself that I don't want to smoke, because of the health risks, and I won't be joining you on smoke breaks anymore. I still like you and want to keep dating." Dan storms off in a huff. However, later, when he thinks it through, he realizes that Jane was honest and mature in her statement. He is able to accept this about Jane and even think about quitting smoking himself.

Conclusion

Thank you for making it through to the end of *Body Language and Non-verbal Communication: The Ultimate Guide for Reading People. Body Language and Non-verbal Communication Will Have No More Secrets for You*! Let's hope it was informative and able to provide you with all of the tools you need to achieve your goals whatever they may be.

The next step is to apply these concepts in your daily life and make observations. Just remember, this might be the first step. As you grow more aware of the psychological principles that are happening around you, you will be more powerful in your inner life and also in relationships.

CPSIA information can be obtained
at www.ICGtesting.com
Printed in the USA
BVHW041748220621
610214BV00012B/2479